RedRaw

poems by

Ali Meyung

Finishing Line Press
Georgetown, Kentucky

RedRaw

Copyright © 2025 by Ali Meyung
ISBN 979-8-88838-869-3 First Edition
All rights reserved under International and Pan-American Copyright Conventions. No part of this book may be reproduced in any manner whatsoever without written permission from the publisher, except in the case of brief quotations embodied in critical articles and reviews.

ACKNOWLEDGMENTS

Thank you to Michelle Naka Pierce, Amy Bobeda, K Blasco Solér, and the Pillowbook Collective. Love and gratitude to my mother, my grandmothers, and ancestors (blood and chosen).

Publisher: Leah Huete de Maines
Editor: Christen Kincaid
Cover Art: Ali Meyung
Author Photo: Ali Meyung
Cover Design: Elizabeth Maines McCleavy

Order online: www.finishinglinepress.com
also available on amazon.com

Author inquiries and mail orders:
Finishing Line Press
PO Box 1626
Georgetown, Kentucky 40324
USA

Contents

Scalpel 1

body-house-cosmos 6

PERIOD 7

Marilyn Monroe 9

Puts Herself Back Together Again 10

Hand Holding 11

(in the light of a dark moon) 12

iud 13

Ovumnal 14

second menarche 16

waiting 17

Ancient Amphora 18

Salomé and the Seven Veils 19

Endnotes 21

Scalpel

It starts in the navel. Searing sizzling pain from deep inside. Wash it, they say, it traps bacteria. I do, I say. No, like really get in there, they say. Okay, I say. I only say okay because I already know this ends with a scalpel and I'm not ready yet.

Nothing changes. That's weird, they say, and they shrug. I'm still not ready.

I begin to track it exactly. Swelling every new moon. Push the lumpy bumpy bellybutton for a yowl, you don't even need a quarter.

It must be the IUD, they say. The doctor has to put their foot up on the medical table below the stirrups for extra leverage to get the little copper horned creature out. When it finally releases, metal embedded with hunks of my insides, the doctor hits the wall behind them with a thud. We've never seen one quite like that before, they say.

The navel still swells and bumps, and I still yowl. Ultrasound required to confirm even though I can roll them between two fingers like pistachios. CT scan reveals nothing we don't already know: I am full of lumps. They are in my urinary tract. Whole torso riddled. A thousand little stars blooming across my guts, throughout my lungs.

My maternal grandmother died in 1971 from an extremely rare lung disease called Lymphangioleiomyomatosis, LAM for short. LAM to make it easier to swallow. LAM to make it tolerable, less intimidating. LAM is not a soft and cute wooly baby that bahs when she's hungry. LAM is tiny little muscular cysts that multiply unchecked all over your lungs. They pop and burn and eat your lungs until you need fresh ones, which is the only cure. While you wait for a new pair, your lungs deflate and air fizzles out in a never-ending dog whistle while they rush you to some country hospital in Missouri. The doctors love you. Never seen in a textbook. See how up close the cysts look like blood globules, but when we back away, you're an entire galaxy of constellations? An objet d'art in a big city like Manhattan; a pièce de résistance in Vandalia, Missouri.

LAM is extremely rare. There are currently 2000 known cases among women of childbearing age across the entire planet. That is less than .0000002% of the population. In all of known medical history, less than ten men have had this disease. It is both discriminatory and genetic. Almost nothing is known about the mechanics and origins of LAM except its relation to tuberculosis sclerosis and that estrogen and progesterone are involved in cyst proliferation, migration, and metastasis.

translation, n.: *Medicine.* Transfer of disease or disease-causing material from one part of the body to another; an instance of this. Obsolete. First use: 1541

My grandmother died age 36. The question becomes, did she translate LAM to me?

When I go under, I'm talking about Beyoncé. They cut me open at the umbilicus, a swirl of an incision. I am riddled with endometrial lesions and scar tissue. Great bloody masses everywhere. uncountable. They shave my abdominal fascia down as lean as possible, pink transparent rice paper. A quality butcher slices deli thin. Even so, they cannot get all the lesions; they penetrate through the fascia and into my guts. Freddy Kruger nightmare massacre carcass. sticky. They sew me back up. When I wake, my mother is telling me to stop talking about how I now understand Michael Jackson's obsession with Propofol.

They tell me everything is okay because they made sure the incision matches the natural whirl of my belly button.

Eighteen hours later the abdominal local wears off and my own screaming wakes me up. I am on the floor, and I cannot uncurl; you need fascia to do that. My lip bleeds where bitten in sleep. Carpet on concrete floor; my skin rubs raw at the hips where I have thrashed against it. My arms are the only parts that I can make work, and I am able use them to hoist myself back up onto the bed. Eventually my mom wakes up and brings me Percocet and wedges a fresh ice pack between my thighs and belly. I slip back under for two days. dreamless.

Nothing left for Freddy Kruger to gouge. My mom brings me drugs at the proper intervals and makes me drink a half liter of water at a time.

My doctors provide me with peer-reviewed articles about thoracic endometriosis. There are likely endometrial lesions spanning the entirety of my insides, but the lungs are the main area of concern. I read the articles. The classic view of endometriosis is that the uterus 'accidentally' sheds menstrual blood out through fallopian tubes and into the body cavity. They call this 'retrograde menstruation.' The retrograde theory accounts for a more typical translation of endometrium when it covers the outside of the reproductive organs in the pelvis. This theory does not explain why and how I am covered with random spots of menstrual blood throughout my entire body. My fallopian tube bled into my lungs? My fallopian tube bled into my brain-blood barrier? No, this disease translated some other way.

But let's spend money on making cocks hard instead.

I can stand up straight again, unfurl my body from empty Percocet space. I am given seven days and nights to heal and to read statistics and data about my diagnosis. I eat only plain foods, lifeless foods: saltines and flavorless bananas. I am not supposed to smoke weed but I am not supposed to bleed all over my insides either, so fuck 'em. The Percocet makes me vomit, and heaving bellies are no asset to flimsy fascia. On the eighth day, I drag my cadaver back to another doctor's appointment.

They bring in a little briefcase, unsnap it and show me the gargantuan spring-loaded needle. I let out a Holy Shit and ask if the mini briefcase says 'ACME' on it. The nurse doesn't get the joke. She grips my ass cheek so hard between her long claws that I yelp, and she unloads a dose of forced ersatz menopause into my ham hock. Lupron Depot. While it turns out my grandmother did not translate LAM to me, had Lupron existed in the late 60s, she also would have received this injection. Discovered and patented in 1973, Lupron stops base body function, forcing my pituitary gland to cease all communication with the rest of my body for the next six months. And even when my pituitary lights back up, I will remain amenorrheic for the next seven years. For your well-being, they say.

Just clean your bellybutton better, they say.

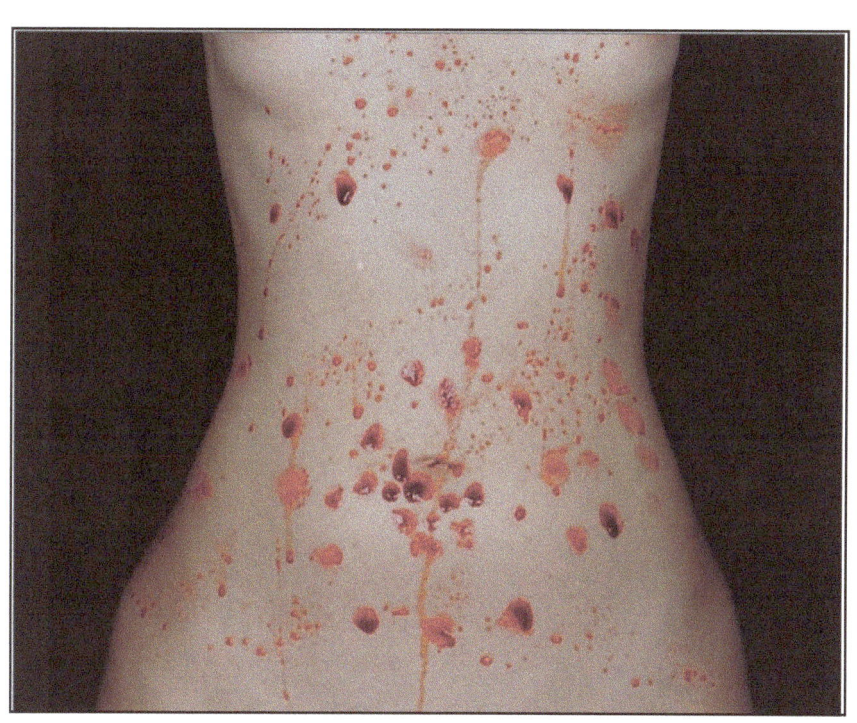

body-house-cosmos
       (endometriosis)

Little star lesions eddy and whorl:
elliptical   irregular   peculiar
lenticular   Spiral connection ancient
Navel cluster triggers detection

Lacerations ubiquitous   embed deep riddle core
suspend craters of offense who dance-strut
the pink ether of my lungs   Embryonic scar systems
amass arrested menorrheic galaxies   Every pit

a ritual wound   every paradise found
every capitulation   coagulates nebulously
Athena punishes Medusa   Lady Artemis hounded
Jocasta hangs   at whose hand?

Laden carriages sink on milky byways
Let us shed burdens betwixt the legs of Perseus

PERIOD

I am a mushroom.
A breeding body.
Or a dormant endoscope.
Petri dish me.
Agar my spores.

Lupron.
Inject. Spring-loaded needle.
Fill petri dish.
Resting body hardens over.
Build a shell.
Resistant to these unfavorable.
Conditions.
But not resistant to heat.
Heat flashes all night.
Dripping the backs of my knees.
I become a sclerotium.
Hardened over *dormant fungus.*
I remain in these unfavorable conditions.
For six months.
Two injections.

Progesterone.
Comes in 21-day packs.
Skips the last week of sugar pills.
Pop small blue pill.
Into my dish each night.
A softening of the hardened.
Sclerotium shell.
Not quite anamorph.
An asexual body.
A breeding body.
Fungi reproduce asexually.
By fragmentation, budding.
Or producing spores.
I am not budding,
Not producing.

I am fragmenting.
Scattering sloughings of skin.
Around me.
Fragments of hyphae.
Can grow new colonies.
Sloughing little fragments.
Everywhere.

Marilyn Monroe

They ask me why I love you.
I could say you are a great actor.
They won't believe me. I say you're funny.
They believe this even less. So I say:

You persist in scattering moonlight.
Ah, this they swallow. Always faint.
Hair stuck up like hay. Pursed lips.
Shaken hips, scattering silver nitrate.

So scattered, you're even missing pieces. Gall bladder
for sure. Uterus, perhaps? Heart, who knows?
But I do love you. Face down, brutally stiff.
Frozen and blissful. Late and sedate.

You split me into numberless infinities of souls
& to your scattered moonlit body, I must go.

Puts Herself Back Together Again

Scalpel loiters sternum, springs open ribs.
Lateral slices & handfuls of sturdy T-pins:
nickel-plated, used for flaps of skin,
for articulating & positioning limp limbs.

Peel back / misfitted / dissection fixed.
Her eyes dilated plates of scattered night,
swallowing her infinitely exposed cadaver
above & behind mirrored surgical light.

Her voice, an echo: *I can do it! Let me try!*
Languid bloated stiff dead fingers rise,
fumble forceps, reach for needle suture.
Recompose / self-stitch / here we linger.

See her open throated rattling breath,
so who she feeds shall dine on death.

Hand Holding

Dolly : Elvira. Inanna : Erishkegal.
Judith : Abra. Demeter : Baubo.

Am I Dolly or Elvira? Is Marilyn shadow or light?
Am I out of my league when I couplet our bodies?

How to distinguish flesh bag from flesh temple?
One drinks moonlight blackhole; other scatters it?

Both performances, pantomimes.
Curling womb wounds prod present.

Push identity, mouth as mace
consume mountain of portrayal.

Labrys splits
voice from throat.

She walks lopsided. Body speaks. Listen.
Perkdog my ear to the great below.

She seeks sympathy, scruffy head in lap
But sew her up sparkling, teeter her on stage

She is one gilded column. I the other. Ruins.
Holding nothing / flanking everything.

See the whole cosmic egg between us
plucked out by Dr Hands in vinyl gloves.

I'll break the plaster / span
threshold to hold her hand.

in the light of a dark moon…

    sangue de guida fizzles crab apple roots burgundy black

    tobacco petals peel sweet

    clumpy blood smears thigh

    hori hori slices datura throats

    snip linden / drench in vodka / bless sleeping mysteries nipples blink

    belladonna buds droop heavy / promise black pool eyes

    little heavenly boats glide Venetian glass water / Luisa Casati's leopards shadow growl

    tart cherries overflow bowls

iud

i want to dirt bleed immemorial
i want to fuck and only make wet
i want to cycle witch and moon
i want to cooper sovereign womb

i want low teen birth rates
i want universal body care
i want skin on skin
i want holy red tend

inside writhing sprawled on floor
inside stuck   doctor two feet up
inside yank   eating mired

inside poison seep tired
inside waging systemic war
inside must come out once more

Ovumnal, *adj.* and *n.*

A. *adj.*
    1. When something is perfectly, sort of round.
        i. 412   HYPATIA   I suggest the earth orbits the sun in an ovumnal pattern.
    2. When something possesses an abstract quality that beckons you to hold it in yr mouth.
        i. 249   ST APOLLONIA   Even though all my teeth have been pulled, that flower still incites an ovumnal feeling when I look at it.
    3. When something creates a confoundedness in yr soul which somehow precipitates new understanding.
        i. 1429   JEANNE D'ARC   I do not know from hence these ovumnal messages appear, but I know I must listen.

B. *Figurative*
    1. Often in terms of books, work, etc.: When a work causes yr body to stop short & feel the vibrations of underworld rivers & hear chthonic deity whispering.
        i. 1988   ANNE WALDMAN   Diane Wolkstein's work translating Inanna myths with Kramer creates a breathlessly ovumnal work for all.
    2. Often in terms of books, work, etc.: When a work can be infinitely folded / unfolded / refolded / crumpled.
        i. 2021   RENEE GLADMAN   Gilles Deleuze's work is *almost* everything he suggests in *The Fold*, very nearly ovumnal, but he ruins it with his seminality.
    3. Often in terms of books, work, etc.: When you try to peel pages apart & they are stuck together with goopy red threads.
        i. 2023   ALI MEYUNG   Amy Bobeda's *Red Memory* bursts with ovumnal pages. Consider purchasing a Diva Cup before reading.

C. *n. Obsolete*
    1. A vessel.
        i. 777   CHARLEMAGNE   We should probably rape and murder all of these ovumnals before they threaten my giant cock.

2. An object resembling either a whole egg or a particle of egg.
    i. 1997   AUSTIN POWERS   Dr. Evil enjoys decorating his evil underground lair with chairs and furniture resembling ovumnals.

second menarche

I eat cherries on someone else's couch.
Tooth sink ripe. Ruby juices lavish.
I scrub someone else's cushion with Dawn.
What if they think it's blood.

I go pee on someone else's toilet.
I wipe and I am eleven again.
Thirty-three. Icky brown mess.
Total blank mind rust surprise.

On the solstice I asked to be cracked open.
Unintended blood invocation. Bing bite
the seven gates of the great below.

Stewed cherry clumps purse purple lips.
Smeared thighs   smeared fingertips.
floatsink great crescent ship.

waiting

no moon today
no spotted crotch
always wondering
              is this it
my grape now a raisin?

others pray for this
trade anything for this
bargain it all away

so many say
          sorry you
          have to go through this
          every month
others laugh when
          i make jokes
          abt freeballin' my endo

i just want to
          pool dirt
          blood
crack open the earth
                like the blade
                of my hori hori
soil swallow
          clumps
          red river
          thigh

perch calendar

bated
          tenterhooks
                no breath

ancient amphora

    body \ vessel   v   womb / vessel
    fallow \ vessel   e s   cunt / vessel
    sonnet \ vessel   s   mouth / vessel
    funerary \ vessel   e l   blood / vessel

    Aphrodite   narrow neck   curved / holy
    unearthed wax ancient   seal easy / tough
    bow low \ wrap lips round earthen mouth
        tongue   longslow   teeth perch cork

lift \ vessel   tip \ vessel   passage / vessel
        burnished clumps   slosh / vessel
          old wine old bread   old moon
                drench hoary /vessel
                   \ still /
                    \vessel/

Salomé and the Seven Veils

Every Friday night for the past seven years, Salomé dances the dance of the seven veils for the Seven Gents at The Seven Tents Nightclub. She takes home seven coins which feed her for the next seven days and nights. No one taught her the dance. But she does not *know* it. It knows her, and you're either born with it or not. Perhaps your bones and muscles wave in time with the lightest and richest fabrics. Perhaps your body ripples oceanscape beneath silken ether. Perhaps your skin unfurls threads of time into moonlight wisps. Or perhaps not.

Once remembered, a sacred dance should never be exploited for monetary gain but after that business with the water obsessed preacher fella, a girl only has so many options, and Salomé knows her innate talent to be rare.

Some nights the dance is sacred and comes from deep within her belly. Other nights it is rote, a bodied ghost. Either way, the music always starts with the slow rattle of a drum. This night, Salomé peeks her thigh out from many layers of material and jerks its meat to the rolling beat. She waves her arms through the tent's thick smoke. Fuses to the music. Coils skin around bones. Wind tussles tent walls. Torches flicker. Hairs stand on end. The beat creeps. Goblets glimmer. Stale smells waft sweet. She inhales the music. Trances her belly into swirling motions, sears blood, flushes languid skin. Sweat slaps. Veils peel and flutter to the floor like dead snakeskin. She twirls and twirls, forever reaching for her rattling tail and never quite grasping it. The tent blurs around her, colors mesh hazy. Stomach flies up. Feet bear down into the sand so she can lift her throat for air. Gasp. Drip, sweat, drip. Thick. Stop.

The drum halts. The last quivering beat hangs in the air, and Salomé freezes, her pinky inger clasped around the drum's dying reverberation. The warble in the music lingers longer than usual. Salomé uses the time to catch her breath. Behind her, Tigellinus gently plucks at his sitar, a rumble that reminds Salomé where she is in the dance. This is her cue to slink out of her sixth and penultimate veil. She rolls the knot at her shoulder between two fingers and watches the diaphanous sheen of silk drift down in the torchlight. A shock of cool air breezes across her sweat-soaked ass.

Oh no. She doesn't dare look down. She knows this breeze must mean she's already stripped bare. *Fuck.* She's not supposed to be nude until the next veil! How did she get ahead of herself? She moves her body and wracks her brain, counting the veils littering the sand. There are only six. As there should be. But there should also be another veil wrapped around her body and here she is stark naked before a crowd of confused men counting on their fingers. How did this happen? She remembers her cat, Wayne, playing with the tasseled fringe of the veils before she came to dance. He must have scampered off with one. *Fuck.* What to do? The punishment for dancing the dance of seven veils with only six is stoning. She continues to sway as if she still teases a veil and pretends she isn't naked. One or two in the crowd attempt to applaud. Others scoot to the edges of their cushions, realizing they might witness both a dance and a stoning in the same evening. She sees a few men reaching into their pockets, feeling for hunks of limestone and granite.

She has no choice.

Salomé reaches her hands up behind her head and digs her nails in at the top of her spine. She peels her skin off in one large rind.

Endnotes

Page 2   *translation definition* from: "Translation." Oxford English Dictionary. Online Edition.

Page 5   Photo by A Meyung

Page 6   Title a reference to: Eliade, Mircea. *The Sacred and the Profane: The Nature of Religion*. Harcourt, Inc. 1987.

Page 7-8   Italics in the Lupron stanza are from: "The Shroomery Mushroom Glossary." Shroomery, www.shroomery.org/glossary.php.
Italics in the Progesterone stanza from: Boundless. "24.1C: Fungi Reproduction." Libre Texts Biology. www.bio.libretexts.org/@go/page13599.

Page 9   'Persists in scattering moonlight':
Mailer, Norman. *Marilyn*. Grosset & Dunlap, 1973.

'you numberless infinities / Of souls, and to your scattered bodies go': Donne, John. 'At the round earth's imagined corners (Holy Sonnet 7),' *Poets.org*, https://poets.org/poem/round-earths-imagined-corners-holy-sonnet-7.

Page 10   'I can do it! Let me try!':
Marilyn Monroe, actor. *The Misfits*. United Artists, 1961.
'so who she feeds shall dine on death':
Derivative of:
The High Priestess Enheduanna. "Lady of the Largest Heart." *Inanna, Lady of Largest Heart, Poems of the Sumerian High Priestess Enheduanna*, by Betty De Shong Meador, 2000, p.121.

Page 14   All quotes are fictitious.

Ali Meyung holds an MFA from the Jack Kerouac School of Disembodied Poetics at Naropa University, where she currently serves as adjunct faculty and associate director of the Writing Center. She also lectures at the University of Colorado in Boulder. She is a martial artist, educator, artist, cat & glitter lover from Denver, Colorado.

www.ingramcontent.com/pod-product-compliance
Lightning Source LLC
Chambersburg PA
CBHW040308170426
43194CB00022B/2949